Card Basics

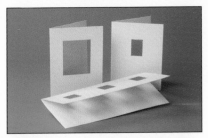

1. Begin with window cards.

2. Ink or stamp front of card.

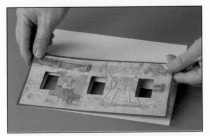

3. Cover card with papers.

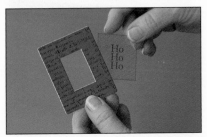

4. Add transparencies to mounts.

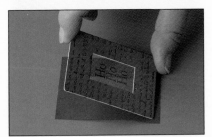

5. Mat mount with cardstock.

6. Add an eyelet or brad to the mount for a decorative touch.

Create something unique and beautiful in less than an hour!

Special gifts deserve unique cards.

Let Dad know how special he is with a card that says "I care enough to make it myself".

Father Gift Card
by Diana McMillan

MATERIALS: *Design Originals* (Printed Mount #0981 Diamonds; Transparency sheet #0625 Memories) • *Adornments* fibers • Tan cardstock • Black sticker letters • Blue *Magic Mesh* • Zots 3-D by *ThermOWeb* • Adhesive

INSTRUCTIONS: **Card:** Cut cardstock 3" x 6". Fold in half. • Add mesh. • **Mount:** Adhere transparency in mount. Wrap fibers and secure to the back.
Add "dad" letters. Adhere with Zots 3-D.

Happy Birthday
by Delores Frantz

MATERIALS: *Design Originals* (Window Card #0992 Small ⬛️⬛️⬛️ ⬛️nt #0987 Vintage Books) • Moss Green cardstock • Vellum • 8 Silver eyelets • *M* ⬛️⬛️⬛️ abet Charms • ⅛" hole punch • Eyelet tools • E6000 • Glue stick

INSTRUCTIONS: **Card:** Cut Moss Green cardstock 4" x 5¼". Cut a w⬛️⬛️ ⬛️htly larger than the card window. Glue to card front. • **Mount:** Use eyelets to attach large mount and 4 tags to card. • **Finish:** Glue letter charms to tags. • Use a computer to print words on vellum. Glue vellum over card window on the inside of the card front.

Sisters Forever

by Michele Charles

Make your card "interactive" with a pull strip. Window cards are perfect for designing pull strips.

MATERIALS: *Design Originals* (Window Card #0994 Three windows; Transparency sheet #0622 Beauties) • Cardstock (Parchment, Manila) • Old book pages • Old sheet music • Crocheted cotton lace • Copper eyelets • Ribbon • Buttons • Gold micro beads • *Limited Edition* miniature girl images • *Stampers Anonymous* #J3-976 text • *JudiKins* dusters • *Craf-T* Decorating Chalk • *ColorBox* Vivid! Tea Rose ink • Ranger ink (Butterscotch reinker, Distress Vintage Photo) • *Posh Impressions* Gold metallic marker • Paint brush • Eyelet tools • Craft knife • *Crafter's Pick* The Ultimate! glue

INSTRUCTIONS: **Background**: Glue torn pieces of old book pages and sheet music to front side of window card. Brush glue tinted with Butterscotch on back and front of pieces. Brush on color heavier in some places than others. Let dry. • **Edges**: Trim paper from card edges and windows. • Use dusters to stipple Vintage Photo ink around the edges of each window. • Line outside edges of card and edges of windows with Gold marker. • **Pull strip**: Cut Manila cardstock 1¾" x 9". Trace and cut out windows. • Glue transparency images behind windows on pull strip. • Cut out "Friend" transparency. Back with Parchment. Glue below the Sisters transparency on pull strip. • Stamp girl images in Vintage Photo ink. Color background with chalk. • Tear top edge. Ink top portion with Vintage Photo. Tie a ribbon through a large button. Glue buttons and micro beads to top. • **Finish**: Cut a 1⅞" wide slit ¼" above the top window on card and slide in pull strip. • Glue on lace. • **Inside card**: see page 7.

1. Trace card windows on Manila strip. Cut out windows.

2. Glue transparencies behind windows on the pull strip.

3. Cut a 2¼" wide slit ¼" above the top window

• •

Life is a Daring Adventure

by Judy Claxton

If you haven't tried combining transparency film with cards, you've got to try this one. It's so easy to get a great effect. Look at the tag, and the corner under the tag for inspiration.

MATERIALS: *Design Originals* Collage papers (#0603 Checkerboard, #0591 US Map, #0548 Passport; Transparency sheets #0561 Travel, #0624 Art Words) • Cardstock (Black, Tan) • Rubber stamps (*JudiKins* Checkered Border 1774G;

Postmodern Design Eiffel CL1-107G, Stamp/Cancel FR1-104D; *Stampers Anonymous* Border U4-970; *Tin Can Mail* Wonderful Time B59-712) • 2 Tan eyelets • Black scrapbook nail • Black wire • Tag • Acetate • *Artchix* Woman with Butterfly Wings • Gold foil corner • Game piece • Fine Line Gold embossing powder • *Krylon* Gold pen • *Adirondack* dye ink (Oregano, Mushroom) • *Tsukineko* StazOn Black dye ink pad • *ColorBox* ink (Creamy Brown Fluid Chalk, Gold pigment) • Eyelet tools • Heat gun • Sponge • Mounting Tape • Glue stick

INSTRUCTIONS: **Card**: Cut Black cardstock 6½" x 10½". Fold in half. Use Gold ink to stamp the Stampers Anonymous Border. • Cut Map paper 4¾" x 6". Ink with Creamy Brown. Edge with Gold pen. • **Collage**: Tear a narrow piece of Passport paper. Stamp with JudiKins checkered border and Oregano ink. Glue to Map paper. • Cut a 9 square block from Checkerboard paper. Gold emboss Eiffel tower. Cut out transparency images and glue to checkerboard upper right corner. • **Small Tag**: Sponge edges of tag with Black ink. Glue "Life is a daring adventure" transparency to tag. Stamp Cancel image on transparency with Black. Adhere tag to checkerboard with scrapbook nail. Glue checkerboard to Map paper. • **Title**: Stamp "wonderful time" on Tan cardstock. Cut ⅝" x 3⅝". Set eyelets. Thread wire through eyelets. Wrap around Map paper. Tape wire ends on the back of the Map paper. Glue Map paper. to card. **Finish**: Cut out woman with butterfly wings. Lightly sponge with Mushroom ink. Outline with Gold pen. Adhere to card with mounting tape. Glue game piece and Gold foil crown in place.

Fabulous Dimension!

By the Sea
by Judy Claxton

Want to make a charming vintage looking card? All you need are chalk ink pads and an image from a vintage postcard.

MATERIALS: *Design Originals* (Collage papers #0589 At the Beach; Mount #0988 Small White; Transparency sheet #0620 Seaside) • Cardstock (Beige Confetti, Coral) • Bathing Beauties vintage postcard • Small seashells • Iridescent shreds • Gold starfish charm • *Tin Can Mail* Palm Tree stamp #H59-561 • *ColorBox* Fluid Chalk ink (Rose Coral, Ice Jade, Creamy Beige, Bisque) • *Krylon* Gold leafing pen • Sponge • *Tombow* Mono Multi Liquid glue • Glue stick
INSTRUCTIONS: **Card**: Cut Beige Confetti cardstock 6" x 11". Fold in half. • Cut Coral mat 5¾" x 5¼". • Stamp card and mat with palm tree border using Creamy Beige ink. Glue Coral to card. • **Collage**: Tear out "sand dunes with sea" and "Queen of Beaches" from At the Beach paper. Sponge with Creamy Beige. Glue to card. Blend the sky to the torn edge by sponging Ice Blue, Rose Coral and Yellow Ochre. • **Mount**: Sponge the mount like the sky. Edge mount with Gold leafing pen. • Adhere the transparency to the back of the mount. Glue mount to the card. • **Finish**: Tear around bathing beauties postcard. Sponge edges. Glue to seaside background. • Use Tombow glue to adhere shreds, seashells, and starfish charm.

From A to Z
by Michele Charles

A to Z features interesting techniques - One, your transparency images will stand out more if you color the back with gesso. Two, embossing can alter a charm to fit your theme.

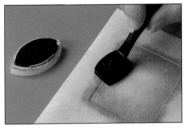

1. Apply Sepia ink to window edges with stylus.

2. Paint the back of the transparency image with Gesso.

3. Cut out the image and adhere to the mount.

MATERIALS:
Design Originals (Window Card #0993 Large window; Collage paper #0578 Vintage ABCs; Printed Mount #0987 Vintage Books; Transparency sheet #0621 Children) • Crocheted cotton lace • *American Art Stamp* image #KC9005T • Metal cameo charm • Embossing ink • Gold embossing powder • *Golden* Gesso • *Ranger* (Vintage Photo Distress ink; Glossy Accents glue) • *ColorBox* (Pigment ink: Gold, Peacock, Chianti, Sepia; Black Fluid Chalk ink; Stylus) • Small paintbrush • Heat gun • Foam tape • Glue stick
INSTRUCTIONS:
Window: Using a stylus, apply Gold ink directly through the window onto the inside of the card. • Use a stylus to ink the edges of the window with Sepia. • **Card Front**: Ink card edges with Sepia. Apply Peacock and Chianti inks to card front only. • Collage edges of card with torn pieces of ABCs paper. • Glue lace to bottom edge of card. • **Mount**: Cut out transparency image. Paint over only the girls and dolls with Gesso. Let dry. Adhere to back of mount. Attach to front of card over window with foam tape. • **Inside card**: Create a mask for the square colored area. Using Vintage Photo ink, stamp image. • Shadow colored box and collaged papers with Black fluid chalk and a small paint brush. • **Finish**: Stamp and emboss the letter "a" in Gold in the center of the metal cameo charm. Cover with Glossy Accents glue. Let dry. Attach to bottom left corner of mount.

Fun, Easy and Quick to Make!

A Photo Christmas
by Delores Frantz

Make personalized Christmas cards using a family photo. Pre-made window cards make it quick, easy and fun!

MATERIALS: *Design Originals* (Window Card #0993 Large window; Collage paper #0579 ABCs Dictionary, #0595 Vintage Script; Printed Mount #0986 Color Game; Transparency sheet #0626 Holidays 2) • Navy Blue cardstock • Vellum • *Jesse James* White snowflake buttons (two ⅝", three ¾") • E6000 • Glue stick

INSTRUCTIONS: **Card:** Cut Navy cardstock 4" x 5¼". Cut a window slightly larger than the card window. Glue to card front. • Cut Script paper 3¾" x 5". Cut a window slightly larger than the Navy cardstock. Glue to card front. • **Mount:** Glue photo and transparency back to back. Glue photo in window. Glue mount over transparency inside card. • **Finish:** Cut "M" from ABCs paper. Mat with Navy Blue cardstock. • Computer print greeting on vellum, with the matted "M" being the first letter of Merry Christmas. Cut vellum 4" x 5¼". Glue "M" to vellum. Glue inside card.

Imagine, Create, Inspire
by Delores Frantz

Need a ready-to-go frame? Consider using printed mounts. Add yet another dimension with eyelets and fibers.

MATERIALS: *Design Originals* (Window Card #0994 Three windows; Collage paper #0596 Maps On Script; Printed Mounts #0987 Vintage Books; Transparency sheet #0624 Art Words) • Black cardstock • 60"

Black 1 mm cord • *Krylon* Silver Leafing Pen • 12 Silver eyelets • ⅛" hole punch • Eyelet tools • Adhesive tape • Glue stick • Ruler

INSTRUCTIONS: **Card:** Using ruler as a guide, apply Silver to edge of card. Cut Black cardstock 3¾" x 8¾". Glue to card front. • Cut Maps paper 3½" x 8½". Glue to Black cardstock. From inside card front cut out windows. • **Mount:** Tape transparencies to the back of the mounts. Set eyelets in corners of mounts. Thread cord through eyelets. Tie a knot at bottom of each mount. Adhere mounts over card windows.

Decorating the Inside of Layered Cards

Gone Fishin'

by Michele Charles

MATERIALS: see page 28

INSTRUCTIONS: **Card**: Cut Blue Linen 6½" x 8½". Fold in half 4¼" x 6½". Dry brush the inside of the card with White acrylic paint. Set aside to dry. • **Images**: Stamp Big Mouth Bass with Vintage Photo ink. Watercolor paint and cut out the image. • Adhere the Bass image inside the card with glue dots for a 3-D effect.

Sisters Forever

by Michele Charles

MATERIALS: see page 4

INSTRUCTIONS: **Background**: Cut Parchment cardstock to cover inside of card. Score where the fold will be. Glue Parchment in place, keeping glue away from the area for pull strip. • Stamp text in Vintage Photo ink. • Use a duster to stipple Tea Rose and Vintage Photo ink over text area. • **Collage**: Tear a scrap of cardstock 1½" x 8". Tear the ends thinner than the middle. • To glue torn pieces of old book pages and sheet music, brush glue tinted with Butterscotch on back and front of pieces. Brush on color heavier in some places than others. Let dry. • Ink torn edge with Vintage Photo. • Set eyelets. Thread ribbons through eyelets. Tape ribbon ends to the back. Glue the collage piece inside the card.

Sea Journey

by Michele Charles

MATERIALS: see page 24

INSTRUCTIONS: **Inside**: Cut Light Green paper to fit inside of card. Tear right edge of paper. Stamp and age with Vintage Photo ink. Glue to inside of card.

By the Sea

by Michele Charles

MATERIALS: see page 19

INSTRUCTIONS: **Inside card**: Cover entire inside of card with Water Marks paper. Turn card over and cut paper from windows. • Hand write words "by the". • Tear beach bather image from At the Beach paper. Shadow with Black chalk using a small paintbrush. Glue to bottom right corner.

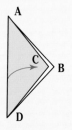

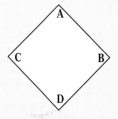

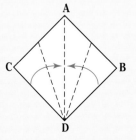

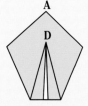

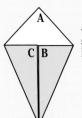

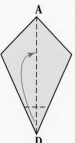

Girls Altered Pages

by Lisa Vollrath

*Looking for a new way to add focus to a photo?
Try surrounding it with a dimensional folded flower.*

MATERIALS: *Design Originals* (Collage papers #0585 Little Girls, #0586 Vintage Flowers; Printed Mount #0984 Vintage Script; Transparency sheet #0621 Children) • Pink cardstock • *Making Memories* Gold star-shaped brads • *Memories* Rose dye ink pad • *Tsukineko* Brilliance Coffee Bean pigment ink pad • Pink printed ribbon • Clear lucite box with lid • Lock of hair • Pink silk ribbon • Pink tag • Letter stamps • Brown embossing powder • Heat tool • Glue stick • Pop Dots

INSTRUCTIONS: **Background**: Cover pages with Pink cardstock. Tear Little Girls paper in half. Glue to left and right page edges. • Tear a piece of Vintage Flowers and glue to top right of layout. • Glue ribbon to page, folding edges around page to finish. **Folded flower**: Cut 8 squares from Vintage Flowers and fold using instructions. Position folded sections on photo, creating a frame. Glue photo and folds to page, trimming photo as necessary. • **Finish**: Adhere transparencies to mounts. Attach to page with Pop Dots. • Apply Rose ink to tag. Stamp title and emboss. Slide tag under corner of large mount. Tie a bow with printed ribbon and anchor in corner of large mount with brad. Add additional brads as desired. Tie lock of hair with small piece of silk ribbon and place in the lucite box. Glue to page.

Making the Folded Flower Sections/Petals

You will need 8 squares.

1. Begin with wrong side of paper facing up and the paper turned so the points are at the top, bottom and sides.

2. Fold paper in half vertically, wrong sides together, matching point C to B. Open back up.

3. Fold the lower sides edges to the center fold line.

4. Your paper should look like this.

5. Turn your paper over and fold point D up so it is even with the side points.

6. Your paper should look like this diagram.

Spirella Pattern
Cut 1 from Pink Cardstock

Kittens and yarn always go together. Make this fun piece of art in a book, or turn this idea into a delightful scrapbook page.

Kitten Altered Book Pages

by Lisa Vollrath

MATERIALS: *Design Originals* Collage paper (#0588 Kittens at Play) • Pink cardstock • *Memories* Burgundy dye ink • Letter stamps • Chenille yarn • *Craf-T* Decorating Chalk • Pop Dots • Glue stick

INSTRUCTIONS: **Background**: Glue Kittens at Play paper to pages. Tear strips of Pink cardstock. Chalk the edges and glue to top and bottom of pages. • **Mat**: Mat photo with Pink cardstock and glue to page. Stamp letters above and below photo.

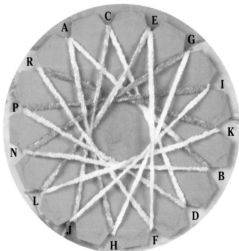

Wind yarn following this easy spirella chart.

• **Spirella**: Cut spirella from Pink cardstock. • Tape beginning of yarn to the back of the spirella. • Wind with chenille yarn in the following pattern, leaving a long tail: A to B, C to D, E to F, G to H, I to J, K to L, B to N, D to P, F to R, H to A, J to C, L to E, N to G, P to I, and R to K. Bring yarn across the back of the spirella so it sticks out at the bottom as in photo and secure in place. • Adhere spirella to the page with Pop Dots. Glue yarn in a winding pattern onto page. Wind a ball of yarn, and wind the end of the tail into the ball. Glue to page.

Layer by Layer Love Cards

Don't wait for a special occasion to appreciate your loved ones. The "Love" cards in this set would be great for Valentine's Day, but they could also be used for a wedding or anniversary, or a romantic note to your beloved. Every mother will appreciate these beautiful "Mom" cards for her birthday or Mother's Day.

All Things Grow with Love
by Donna Kinsey

MATERIALS: *Design Originals* (Window Card #0993 Large window; Collage paper #0586 Vintage Flowers, #0280 Roses and Pearls; Printed Mount #0984 Vintage Script; Transparency sheet #0625 Memories) • *Creative Beginnings* Gold heart charm • *Adornaments* fibers • *Magic Scraps* micro beads • Mini Glue Dots • Red Liner tape
INSTRUCTIONS: **Card**: Cover window card with Roses paper. Tear flowers from Vintage Flowers paper and glue to the inside corner of the card. • **Mount**: Cut mount apart at hinge. Cut transparency slightly larger than the window. Adhere to the back of the mount. • **Finish**: Use mini Glue Dots to adhere mount over window. Cover center opening in heart charm with Red Liner tape. Remove paper. Sprinkle micro beads. Adhere to card with Mini Glue Dots.

What is Love
by Donna Kinsey

MATERIALS: *Design Originals* (Window Card #0993 Large window; Collage paper #0586 Vintage Flowers; #0607 Vellum Sentiments, #0471 Scrappin Red; Mount #0991 Large White) • *Creative Beginnings* Gold rose charm • Scrap of Lace • 3 silk flowers • *Offray* pearl ribbon • *Suze Sparkle* glitter • *Xyron* adhesive • Mini Glue Dots • Pop Up Glue Dots • Glue stick • Brayer
INSTRUCTIONS: **Card**: Cover window card with Red paper. Tear flowers from Vintage flower paper and collage to card. Glue or stitch lace to card. • **Mount**: Cut mount apart at hinge. Run mount through Xyron adhesive. Cover with glitter. Tap to remove excess glitter. Use a brayer to press glitter onto mount. • Cut vellum larger than the window. Adhere to back of mount. • **Finish**: Use mini Glue Dots to adhere mount over window. Add rose charm and silk flowers with Pop Up Glue Dots.

Mom Remembered
by Delores Frantz

MATERIALS: *Design Originals* (Window Card #0993 Large window; Collage paper #0607 Vellum Sentiments) • *ColorBox* Pink ink • *Offray* Pink ribbon • 4 Pink eyelets • *EK Success* Iron Eagle corner punch • Rose cut from Vintage card • Craft knife • Sponge • Glue stick
INSTRUCTIONS: **Card**: Sponge front of card. Punch out bottom corners. • **Vellum**: Tear vellum to cover window. Ink the edges. Attach to card with eyelets. • **Finish**: Glue Rose in place. Cut a small slit in the fold of the card. Thread the ribbon through the slit and the corner punch in the bottom of the card. Tie a bow.

To Mother with Love
by Delores Frantz

MATERIALS: *Design Originals* (Window Card #0993 Large window; Collage paper #0587 Runaway Doll; Printed Mount #0980 Water Marks) • Rose cardstock • 4 Rose eyelets • 24" *DMC* Burgundy pearl cotton • Burgundy butterfly applique • 2" Silver Mother charm • *ColorBox* Cat's Eye Light Red ink • 1/8" hole punch • Eyelet tools • E6000 • Glue stick • Pop Dots
INSTRUCTIONS: **Card**: Cut 2 pieces of Rose cardstock 4" x 5¼". In 1 piece, cut a window to fit the card window. Glue to card front. • Tear a 3¾" x 5" piece from the upper right corner of Doll paper. Apply ink to edges. Trace and cut a window in paper. Center and glue to card front. • **Mount**: Set eyelets in corners of mount. Thread floss through eyelets. Glue floss ends on back of mount. Glue mount over card window. • **Finish**: Glue the second piece of Rose cardstock inside card. • Center and glue Mother charm in window. Use Pop Dots to attach butterfly to upper left side of card.

All things
grow
with
Love

Love
n. A feeling
of strong
personal attachment,
or ties of kinship:
ardent affection.

Mom reaches
for your hand and
touches your heart.

Flowers for Mom
by Christy Gilbreath

No one will ever love you like your Mom. Remember her with this lovely card.

MATERIALS: *Design Originals* (Collage paper #0586 Vintage Flowers; Mount #0988 Small White; Transparency sheet #0557 Family) • *Bazzill* Yellow cardstock • Vellum • *Offray* Pink ribbon • Pink brads • Glue stick • *3M* Vellum tape

INSTRUCTIONS: **Card:** Cut cardstock 6½" x 10¼". Fold in half. • Cut Vintage Flowers paper and glue to front of card. • Tape vellum to the card next to the fold. • **Border:** Tear a strip of cardstock 1¼" x 6⅜". Adhere to card with brads. • **Mount:** Cover mount with Vintage Flowers paper. Tape transparency to the back of the mount. Glue to card. • **Finish:** Wrap ribbon around the card and tie in a bow.

Wisdom with Flair
by Michele Charles

Show your loved one how much you appreciate their wisdom. Create this beautiful card using a transparency sheet beauty, stamps and punches. Special attention is always received with love.

MATERIALS: *Design Originals* Transparency sheet #0622 Beauties • Cardstock (Dark Green, Manila) • Rubber stamps (*Stampers Anonymous* Script; *Non Sequitur* Wisdom) • *EK Success* fleur-de-lis punch • *JudiKins* dusters • *Ranger* ink (Butterscotch, Green) • *Posh Impressions* Gold metallic marker • Gold embossing powder • Heat gun • Foam tape • Glue stick

INSTRUCTIONS: **Card:** Cut Manila cardstock 5½" x 8½". Fold in half. • Stamp script in Green ink. Use duster to stipple Butterscotch all over front of card. Stipple Bottle Green ink around the edges. Edge card with Gold Metallic marker • **Frame:** Cut Dark Green cardstock 3¼" x 4". Cut a 2" x 2½" window in the center. • Line all edges of frame with Gold metallic marker. • Cut image from transparency sheet. Adhere to the back of the frame. Cut a Manila cardstock mat and glue behind the transparency. Adhere frame to card with foam tape. • **Corners:** Rub Gold ink directly on Manila cardstock and emboss with Gold embossing powder. Punch out corner shapes. Glue to corners of frame. • **Title:** Stamp and Gold emboss the word wisdom on Dark Green cardstock. Edge with Gold metallic marker. • Punch out 2 more decorative corners. Cut off point of shape and glue to left and right edges of Wisdom piece. • Glue wisdom piece directly beneath frame on front of card.

Vintage Collage with Printed Mount, Page Pebbles and Stars

Read Books

by Judy Claxton

Get that popular vintage look and show off your love of books at the same time with this collaged card.

MATERIALS: *Design Originals* Collage papers (#0614 ABCs, #0580 School Books, #0579 ABCs Dictionary, #0547 Dictionary; Printed Mount #0987 Vintage Books) • Red cardstock • Magazine image of children reading • *Postmodern Design* (Diamond Bar BL4-110E, Gothic Caps Alphabet large) • 3 Gold stars • *Making Memories* Page Pebbles • Alphabet pieces • *Adirondack* Latte dye ink • Foam dots • Glue stick

INSTRUCTIONS: **Card:** Cut Red cardstock 6" x 12". Fold in half. • Cut School Books paper 5½" x 5½". Glue to card. • **Collage:** Stamp the word BOOKS with Latte ink in the upper left corner of card. • Cut out "A-B-C" from ABCs Dictionary paper. Glue to right side of card. • Tear ABC from ABC paper. Stamp with Diamond bar and Latte ink. Glue to left side of card. • **Mount:** Cut out magazine image of children reading. Place cut-out into mount. • Cut out "round about you" from School Books paper. Tear out dictionary definition. Glue to mount. Attach Page Pebbles to mount. • Adhere mount to card with foam dots. • **Finish:** Glue the Gold stars above the mount.

1. Cut out images.

2. Age letters with ink.

3. Glue in place.

4. Fit photo into mount.

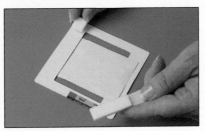

5. Add foam dots to the back of the mount.

6. Glue stars in place.

Report Card
by Judy Claxton

Whether it's the gym shoes, school books, or the bright yellow bus that you remember most, capture your favorite memorabilia in a reminiscent collage.

MATERIALS: *Design Originals* (Collage papers #0577 School Days, #0580 School Books, #0541 Report Card) • Cardstock (Red, Beige Confetti) • Paper (Blue Denim) • Navy ribbon with stars • Rubber stamps (*Stamp Out Cute* Peg Alphabet #4; *Postmodern Design* Captain Slab TR1-101D, High Tops #RE3-110D) • Red stars • Die-cut school bus • Bingo magnet • Red eyelets • String • *ColorBox* Fluid Chalk ink (Warm Red, Creamy Brown) • Sponge • Eyelet tools • Glue stick
INSTRUCTIONS: **Card**: Cut Red cardstock 6¼" x 10½". Fold in half. • Cut Denim paper 4⅞" x 5⅞". • Cut School Days paper 4⅝" x 5⅝". Lightly sponge the corners with Creamy Brown ink. Glue to Denim paper. • Wrap ribbon around the bottom. Tape ends to the back. • **Collage**: Tear "Report Card" from Report Card paper. Sponge with Warm Red and Creamy Brown Fluid Chalks. Glue to background paper. • Glue school bus to background paper. Cut out 2 books from Vintage School Books paper, glue to background paper. • **Finish**: Stamp Hi Tops with Warm Red on Beige Confetti paper. Cut out. Set an eyelet at the top of each shoe. Attach a piece of string in each eyelet and tape behind denim paper. Glue to card. • Glue the stars and bingo magnet to the card. Stamp "important document" from the Captain Slab and "speller" using alphabet in Red.

Creative Designs that Inspire

Asian Lady
by Judy Claxton

The "mysterious East" continues to enchant us with exotic symbols, sense of history and traditions. Collage favorite motifs on this beautiful Asian card.

MATERIALS: *Design Originals* (Collage papers #0600 Dominoes; Printed Mount #0987 Vintage Books) • Cardstock (Golden Confetti, Black, White) • Gold specked mulberry paper • Joss paper • Book board • Large Gold eyelet • Red cord • Asian coin • *Dover* Women from Faraway Places and Times • Rubber stamps (*Postmodern Design* Two Tone EA3-105F; *Acey Deucy* Windswept #932) • *Krylon* Gold pen • *Tsukineko* StazOn Black dye ink • *Marvy* Black marker • *ColorBox* ink (Warm Red Fluid Chalk, Gold pigment) • Eyelet tools • Sponge • Mounting Tape • Glue stick
INSTRUCTIONS: **Card**: Cut Golden Confetti cardstock 6¼" x 10½". Fold in half. • Cut Black cardstock 5" x 6". Glue to card. • **Collage**: Tear dominoes box from Dominoes paper. Rub edges with Gold ink. Glue to card. • Stamp Two Tone image on Black cardstock and mulberry paper. Tear small pieces of mulberry paper and glue to card. • **Small Tag**: Transfer images of Asian women from Dover book to transparency. • Glue Joss, mulberry papers, and small image transparency to small Red tag. • Set eyelet. Add small red cord. Edge tag with Black marker. • **Mat**: Cut book board the desired size for face transparency. Glue Gold portion of Joss paper and transparency to board. Edge with Black marker. • **Coin**: Stamp tag portion of Windswept image with Warm Red ink on a scrap of White cardstock. Cut out and glue to Asian charm. Run Red cord through loop and attach to the top of the card. • **Finish**: Adhere mat to the center of the card with mounting tape. Glue small red tag to the top left of center mat.

Revisit Yesterday with Great Cards

Grandfather

by Delores Frantz

Remember Grandpa on Father's Day with a vintage gaming card.

MATERIALS: *Design Originals* (Window Card #0993 Large window; Collage paper #0600 Dominoes, #0607 Vellum Sentiments; Printed Mount #0986 Color Game) • *Jesse James* metal charm • *ColorBox* Cat's Eye Chestnut Roan ink • Pop Dots • E6000 • Glue stick

INSTRUCTIONS: **Card**: Cut Dominoes paper 4" x 5¼". Cut a window slightly larger than the card window. Glue to card front. • Cut out dominoes from Dominoes paper. Adhere to card with Pop Dots. • **Mount**: Tape Vellum Sentiment to back of mount. Glue inside card centering mount in the window. • **Finish**: Adhere charm with E6000.

Be Mine
by Delores Frantz

Remember the Valentines you exchanged in elementary school? Make a card that brings back those memories and share it with your valentine today. Better yet, make several and send them to those old friends.

MATERIALS: *Design Originals* (Window Card #0992 Small window; Collage paper #0580 School Books, #0481 Teal Linen; Printed Mounts #0982 Game Pieces, #0983 Tapes; Transparency sheet #0623 Games) • *Die Cuts With A View* metal phrase • 6 Black eyelets • ⅛" Hole punch • Eyelet tools • E6000 • Glue stick

INSTRUCTIONS: **Card**: Adhere a 3¾" x 5" piece of Books paper centered on a 4" x 5¼" piece of Teal paper. Adhere to card front and cut windows out. • **Mount**: Adhere transparency to the back of the Tapes mount. Adhere to card front. Set eyelets. • **Finish**: Cut Teal paper mat for metal charm. Adhere charm with E6000. Set eyelets. Glue to front of card. • Glue Game Pieces mount to the inside of the card around the window.

The  Song

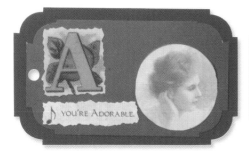

Large and Small Tags with Punched Corners and Holes, Computer Words aged with Chalk, Cut out Letters and Images...

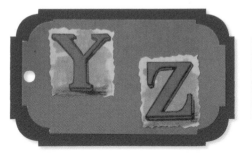

A Song for My Valentine
by Donna Kinsey

Even if you can't sing, you can give your valentine the "Alphabet Love Song" with this tag book.

MATERIALS: *Design Originals* (Collage papers #0578 Vintage ABCs, #0579 ABCs Dictionary, #0586 Vintage Flowers, #0479 Green Stripe, #0480 Green Floral, #0481 Teal Linen, #0482 Teal Stripe, #0483 Teal Floral, #0484 Blue Linen, #0485 Blue Stripe, #0486 Blue Floral, #0487 Rust Linen, #0488 Rust Stripe, #0489 Rust Floral, #0490 Coffee Linen, #0491 Coffee Stripe, #0466 Scrappin Blue, #0467 Scrappin Green, #0468 Scrappin Aqua, #0470 Scrappin Brown, #0471 Scrappin Red; The Ephemera Book #5207; Transparency sheet #0560 Objects) • *Bazzill* 12" x 12" cardstock for large

tags (Burgundy, Royal Blue, Forest Green) • *Mark Enterprises* Alphabet dots • *Creative Beginnings* Gold heart charm • 2" scrap of Red cardstock for heart on "C" page • Feather for "F" page • 1 Copper eyelet for "O P" page. • Drawing of "OK" hand for "S T" page • Picture of a puzzle for "U" page • *Adornaments* fibers • *Westex* Ring it 2½" metal ring • *Marvy* (1" heart punch, corner rounder) • *Craft-T* Decorating Chalk • *Fiskars* Deckle edge scissors • *Xyron* adhesive • Mini Glue Dots • Glue stick

INSTRUCTIONS: **Large tags**: All large tags are cut 3" x 5" and corners are rounded with a corner punch. Here are the numbers and colors to cut: 6 Burgundy, 6 Blue, 9 Green. • **Small tags**: All tags are cut 2½" x 4½" and corners are rounded with a corner punch. • **Assembly**: Mount small tags onto large tags. • Punch holes in tags, making sure the holes line up for all tags. • **Words**: Computer print the words from the "Alphabet Love Song". Age with chalk. Cut out with deckle scissors. • **Images**: Cut out alphabet letters, and coordinating images from the Ephemera book. Choose tag colors to coordinate with the letter and image. • **Embellishments**: On the "C" page, punch a Red heart and write "cutie" with a marker. Attach the heart charm with a glue dot. • **Finish:** Thread tags onto metal ring. Decorate metal ring with fibers.

Sun Fun

by Judy Claxton

Having a great time! Wish you were here. Make a card that takes you to your favorite vacation spot. This realistic pebble beach is made with sandpaper. Add vintage images of bathing beauties for a fun-in-the-sun beach card.

MATERIALS: *Design Originals* (Collage papers #0609 Vellum Passport, #0589 At the Beach, #0549 Shorthand, #0411 Postcards; Mount #0991 Large White; Transparency sheet #0620 Seaside) • Cardstock (White, Beige Confetti) • *Jolee* (flowers, sunglasses) • *Marcel Schurman* Gift Toppers sandals • Coarse grit sandpaper • Rubber stamps (*Stampington* Solstice M4733; *Memories* Date Stamp kit; *Authentic Models* AB Seas Alphabet) • *Krylon* Gold pen • *Angelwings* (Twinkling H2Os: Sunburst, Solar Gold, Gold Dust) • *Tsukineko* StazOn Black dye ink • *ColorBox* Fluid Chalk ink (Creamy Brown, Ice Jade, Warm Red) • Sponge • Glue stick

1. Tear the sandpaper layers.

2. Cut out girl sunbather from paper and sponge with ink.

INSTRUCTIONS: **Card:** Cut Confetti cardstock 6¾" x 11". Fold in half. • **Collage:** Tear sand and sky from At the Beach paper. Glue to cardstock. Sponge ink the sky with Warm Red.• Tear sandpaper in several narrow pieces. Glue to cardstock to resemble beach sand. Cut out female sunbather from At the Beach paper. Sponge with Creamy Brown ink. Glue to the sandpaper. Add a Jolee flower. • **Mount:** Collage mount with bits of Passport vellum, Shorthand paper, and Postcards paper. Sponge with Creamy Brown ink. • Tape transparency to the back of the mount. Glue to card. • Tear "Beach, Cal" from At the Beach paper. Glue to mount. Stamp "Sun" and "Fun" with AB Seas stamps in Black ink. • Stamp "Jun, Jul, Aug" in Warm Red ink with Date Stamp kit. • **Finish:** Glue sandals to card. • Stamp Solstice image on White cardstock. Watercolor with Twinkling H2Os beginning with lighter color and working outward to darker colors. Cut out sun. Edge with Gold pen. Glue sun to card.

By the Sea

by Michele Charles

Embellish your card with items you pick up on the beach. Driftwood, sea stars, and sea glass give your card a recognizable theme and dimension.

MATERIALS: *Design Originals* (Window Card #0994 Three windows; Collage paper #0618 Water Marks, #0589 At the Beach) • 3 pieces of sea glass • Twig • Raffia ribbon • Alphabet stamps • Acrylic paint (Blue, White) • *Folk Art* Crackle medium • *Tsukineko* Black StazOn ink • *ColorBox* Black Fluid Chalk • Hole punch • Craft knife • Foam core board • Glue stick

INSTRUCTIONS: **Inside card**: see p. 7. • **Card front**: Mask window openings from the inside. Paint window card solid blue with acrylic paint. Let dry. • Paint a layer of Crackle medium over the Blue. Let dry. • Gently brush on a layer of White acrylic paint over the dried crackle medium. Do not brush back and forth when applying White acrylic paint; this will cover up the cracks. • **Twig**: Punch four holes and thread raffia ribbon through from backside. Tie on twig. • **Finish**: Cut swimmer from At the Beach paper. Trace around outline on foam core board. Cut foam core board. Ink the edges of the foam core board. Glue image to foam core board. • Hand write words "you and me" on front of card. • Using StazOn ink, stamp the letters S-E-A onto 3 pieces of sea glass. • Glue swimmer and star fish to front of card. • With card closed, glue the sea glass with stamped letters inside the windows of card.

1. Paint card blue.

2. Paint over the crackle medium with acrylic paint.

3. Add embellishments.

Baby Cakes
by Judy Claxton

Vintage photos make interesting focal points for your card. Decorate around them with colors and related ephemera to obtain that popular nostalgic look.

MATERIALS: *Design Originals* Collage papers (#0615 Words, #0616 Spots, #0547 Dictionary) • Cardstock (Dark Beige, Beige Confetti, Black) • Ribbon (5" wide sheer Beige, Check Black and Beige) • Rubber stamps (*Serendipity* Large Clock K446; *Postmodern Design* Med Romantic Swirl BL9-106-D, Precious PL1-104E, Alpha Strip DC2-109D, Sweetie Pie Slab RE1-104-D) • *Tsukineko* ink (StazOn Black, Ancient Page Sienna) • Glue stick
INSTRUCTIONS: **Card**: Cut Dark Beige cardstock 6¾" x 10½". Fold in half. • Cut Black mat 5" x 6½". • Cut Words paper 4¾" x 6¼" and adhere to Black mat. • **Collage**: Tear pieces of Dictionary paper. Sponge with Sienna Ink. • Stamp Large Clock and alphabet with Black ink. Stamp Romantic Swirl with Sienna ink. • Wrap Words paper with sheer Beige ribbon. Tape ends to the back. Glue to card. • **Finish**: Cut Black mat 2⅞" x 4⅜". • Stamp Precious with Black dye ink onto Spots paper. Cut to 2⅝" x 4⅛". Glue to Black mat. • Tie checkered ribbon around bottom. Glue to card. • **Title**: Cut Black mat ⅝" x 2½". Stamp "baby cakes" on a scrap of Light Beige Confetti cardstock. Cut out and glue to Black mat. Glue to card.

Beauty
by Judy Claxton

MATERIALS: *Design Originals* (Collage paper #0535 Ruth's Letter, #0611 Vellum Clocks; Printed Mount #0988 Small White; Transparency sheet #0622 Beauties, #0625 Memories) • Cardstock (Dark Beige Confetti, Pale Pink, Cream) • 3 feathers • Small vintage watch face • Variegated Pink and Cream silk ribbon • Beige eyelets • Pink iridescent sequin remnant • Pink *Magic Mesh* • Rubber stamps (*Stamp Out Cute* Peg Alphabet and Numbers Set #4; *JudiKins* Treasures Cube 6585H) • *ColorBox* Fluid Chalk Creamy Brown ink • *Postmodern Design* Walnut ink • Eyelet tools • *Tombow* Mono Multi Liquid glue • Glue stick
INSTRUCTIONS: **Card**: Cut Dark Beige cardstock 6¼" x 10½". Fold in half. • Cut Vellum Clocks paper 5¼" x 6¼" • Cut Cream mat 5" x 6". Cut Pink mat 4½" x 5½". Stack and glue mats to card. • **Collage**: Stamp Treasures face onto Ruth's letter randomly with Creamy Brown ink. Glue to card. Adhere mesh to bottom of card. Use Tombow to glue sequin remnant to left side of card.• **Mount**: Color mount with a very light coat of walnut ink. Stamp "Sara" and numbers on mount with Creamy Brown ink. • Wrap one side of mount with silk ribbon. • Attach "Beauty" transparency to mount with eyelets. • Tape transparency to the back of the mount. • Glue feathers to back of mount. Glue mount to card.

Sisters – Friends

by Delores Frantz

Here's a fun card for a sewing buddy, quilter, or sister.

Punch holes in mounts, and make a running stitch around the mounts.

Add a needle and thread, charms and a half spool of thread to finish your creation.

MATERIALS: *Design Originals* (Window Card #0994 Three windows; Collage paper #0586 Vintage Flowers; Printed Mount #0982 Game Pieces; Transparency sheet #0622 Beauties) • Forest Green embroidery floss • *Jesse James* charms (needle, scissors) • 3⁄4" Wood spool • Embroidery needle • *ColorBox* Cat's Eye Rose Coral ink • 1⁄16" hole punch • Eyelet tools • E6000 • Glue stick

INSTRUCTIONS: **Card**: Tear Flowers paper 3¾" x 8¾". Cut 3 windows to match card. Apply ink to edges. Glue to card front. • **Mount**: Punch holes ¼" apart along edges of mounts. Use needle to sew a running stitch through punched holes. Adhere transparencies in mounts. Glue mounts over windows. • **Finish**: Cut spool in half. Wrap floss around spool. Glue spool and scissors charm to mounts with E6000. • Thread floss through needle charm. Glue needle charm and floss to mount with E6000.

1. Ink the edges of the paper.

2. Poke holes in the mount with a T pin.

3. Stitch mounts.

Cat Collage Card
by Amy Hubbard

MATERIALS: *Design Originals* (Collage papers #0585 Little Girls Paper, #0587 Runaway Doll, #0588 Kittens at Play; Printed Mount #0981 Diamonds) • Cardstock (Brown, Rose) • *Making Memories* Antique Gold heart paper clip • Pink *Adornments* Fibers • Paper crimper • Mini Glue Dots • Glue stick

INSTRUCTIONS:

Card: Cut Rose cardstock 5½" x 8½". Fold in half. • Cut Brown cardstock 3¾" x 5". Tear strips of Kittens at Play, Little Girls and Runaway Doll paper. Glue to Brown cardstock. • Cut another piece of Brown cardstock 1¼" x 3¾". Crimp and attach to the bottom of Brown cardstock. Tie fibers around the crimped piece. • **Mount**: Tape kitten image to the back of the mount. Attach to Brown panel with Glue Dots. • **Finish**: Attach heart paper clip to the top of the mount with mini glue dots. Thread fibers through the top and tape to the back of the cardstock panel. • Attach the decorated cardstock panel to Pink card.

Love Card
by Diana McMillan

MATERIALS: *Design Originals* (Printed Mount #0981 Diamonds; Transparency sheet #0625 Memories) • Green cardstock • *Nostalgiques* Tea Stained Tag ABC stickers • 4 *Boxer* Gold mini brads • Twine • Heart charm • Memory Tape Runner • Zots 3-D

INSTRUCTIONS: **Card**: Cut cardstock 5½" x 8½". Fold in half. Cut a window in the front of the card 2⅜" x 2⅝". • **Mount**: Adhere transparency to the back of the mount. Wrap twine around mount, threading heart charm onto twine. Secure twine to the back of the mount. Adhere mount to card over window with Zots 3-D. • **Title**: Position stickers. Add brads.

Baby Boy Card — *by Amy Hubbard*

This trio is easily adapted for any occasion. Your favorite cat lover will treasure this pretty "Cat Collage". Celebrate your new arrival with a lovely blue baby announcement. Or, send some appreciation to a soldier far from home with this "Love" card.

MATERIALS: *Design Originals* (Collage papers #0582 Toys for Boys; Mount #0988 Small White; Transparency sheet #0625 Memories) • Blue cardstock • *Memories* Blue dye ink pad • 3 *EK Success* Button Ups • Letter beads • Sponge • Glue stick • Glue Dots

INSTRUCTIONS: **Card:** Cut cardstock 5½" x 8½". Fold in half. • Tear and glue Toys for Boys paper in the corners of the card. • **Mounts:** Sponge mounts with Blue ink. Adhere transparencies in mounts. Glue letter beads in place. Glue mounts to card. • **Finish:** Adhere Button Ups to card.

Golden Lady — *by Delores Frantz*

Gold adds a touch of artistic elegance to any card. These gold photo mounts direct your attention to the Golden Lady at the center.

MATERIALS: *Design Originals* (Window Card #0993 Large window; Printed Mount #0984 Vintage Script) • Navy Blue cardstock • *Amy's Magic* Gold lady charm • 4 Gold picture mounts • 4 Gold eyelets • ⅛" hole punch • Eyelet tools • E6000 • Glue stick

INSTRUCTIONS: **Card:** Cut Navy cardstock 4" x 5¼". Cut window to fit card. • **Mount:** Glue mount over window. Use eyelets to attach picture mounts over corners of mount. • **Finish:** Glue Gold charm to a small rectangle of Navy Blue cardstock. Center and glue inside card so they show through the window.

Sea Journey

by Michele Charles

Wishing you calm seas and gentle breezes, these cards echo the call of the Seven Seas.

Take a Sea Journey with stamped images and transparencies or shout "Bon Voyage" from the main deck as you sail the world on World Stamps paper. Allow yourself a seafaring adventure while making these delightful cards. Then send them out for birthdays, Father's Day, or "just because".

MATERIALS: *Design Originals* (Window card #0993 Large Window; Printed Mount #0982 Game Pieces; Transparency sheet #0620 Seaside) • Dark Green cardstock • Paper (Light Green, Manila) • Seashell • Cameo • Rubber stamps (*Stampers Anonymous* #P1-666 Map Corner; *Serendipity Stamps* #816-532-0740 Script; *Inkadinkado* #90933 Sea Journey) • *Ranger* (Distress Vintage Photo ink; Glossy Accents glue) • *Golden* Gesso • Paintbrush • Foam tape • Glue Dots • Glue stick

INSTRUCTIONS: **Card**: Using window card as template, cut card from Dark Green cardstock. • Stamp Map Corner on Green paper with Vintage Photo ink. Tear stamped image and ink edges with Vintage Photo. Glue to corners of card. • **Mount**: Cut image from transparency. On the back of the transparency, paint the ship area only with Gesso. • Glue transparency to back of mount. Attach to front of card with foam tape. • **Title**: Stamp the letters S-E-A and the word "Journey" with Vintage Photo ink on Manila paper. Tear out words. Ink torn edges with Vintage Photo. Glue to the front of the card beneath mount. • **Finish**: Glue a small transparency image to a cameo piece with Glossy Accents. • Adhere seashell and cameo with Glue Dots.
• **Card Inside:** See page 7.

Sisters Card

by Lisa Vollrath

If you have a sister, she will be having a birthday. Why not send the "sisters" or "ladies" card? Both are sure to please.

If you are planning a trip, make some cards to send home. These fun "Bon Voyage" cards will also give you a start on your travel journal.

MATERIALS: *Design Originals* (Window Card #0994 Three windows; Printed Mounts #0982 Game Pieces, #0983 Tapes; Transparency sheet #0622 Beauties) • *Melanie Sage* Love Letter stamp • *Stampa Rosa* Fresco dye ink pads (Venetian Sunrise, Sicilian Spice, Amaretto Truffle) • 13 *Making Memories* small Gold brads • Black rayon embroidery floss • Awl • Double-sided tape

INSTRUCTIONS: **Card**: Apply Venetian Sunrise and Sicilian Spice inks to card direct to paper. Let dry. Stamp card with Love Letter stamp and Amaretto Truffle ink. • **Mounts**: Tape transparencies to the back of the mounts. Stack mounts and punch holes in four corners with awl. Insert brads into holes. Tape mounts to front of card over windows. • **Finish**: Insert brad into top center of card. Starting at bottom of card, wrap rayon floss around brad in mount, leaving a short tail. Bring up to next brad, and wrap again. Continue wrapping up side of mounts, up to center brad, and down the other side. Tack floss in first and last brad with adhesive if desired. Fray ends of floss and trim to desired length.

Make fun and unusual cards using `Layer by Layer` techniques.

Bon Voyage with Ship

by Delores Frantz

MATERIALS: *Design Originals* (Window Card #0993 Large window; Collage paper #0592 World Stamps; Printed Mount #0982 Game Pieces; Transparency sheet #0619 Travel 2) • Cardstock (Teal, White) • 4 Antique Silver eyelets • 1/8" hole punch • Eyelet tools

INSTRUCTIONS: **Card**: Cut a Teal 4" x 5¼" mat. Cut a window slightly larger than card window. Glue to card front. • Cut a mat 3¾" x 5" from Stamp paper. Cut window slightly larger than the Teal mat. Glue to card front. • **Mount**: Tape transparency to back of mount. Glue inside card centering mount in the window. • **Finish**: Place White cardstock behind Bon Voyage transparency. Mat on Teal cardstock. Set eyelets in corners. Glue to card front.

Ladies

MATERIALS: *Design Originals* (Window Card #0993 Large window; Transparency sheet #0622 Beauties) • 4 Pink eyelets • *Adornments* fibers • *EK Success* corner punch • Eyelet tools

INSTRUCTIONS: **Card**: Punch all 4 corners with a decorative corner punch. • **Window**: Trim transparency slightly larger than the window opening. Set eyelets to hold transparency in place. • **Finish**: Loop fibers through the fold in the card. Tie a knot.

Bon Voyage Card

by Lisa Vollrath

MATERIALS: *Design Originals* (Window Card #0992 Small window; Printed Mount #0987 Vintage Books; Transparency sheet #0619 Travel 2) • *Making Memories* Silver star-shaped brads • *Inkadinkado* Postoid stamps • *Memories* Black dye ink pad • Old postage stamps • *Xyron* adhesive • Double-sided tape

INSTRUCTIONS: **Card**: Run transparencies through Xyron. Arrange on card as desired. Adhere sin place. • **Mount**: Tape Bon Voyage transparency to back of mount. Attach to card over window with brads. • **Finish**: Fill the empty spots on the card with postage stamps and stamped postoids.

Dreamy Eyes Tag Card

by Michele Charles

Petrarch summed up the effect of beautiful eyes when he said "The eyes that drew from me such fervent praise...". You are sure to receive similar praise when you make this beautiful card. The eyes on this card are on a fun pull-out tag which can be used as a bookmark later.

MATERIALS: *Design Originals* (Collage paper #0595 Vintage Script) • Cardstock stock (Black, Cream) • *Making Memories* Alphabet Page Pebbles • Black tassel • *Creative Beginnings* Gold heart charm • Rubber stamps (*Stampers Anonymous* small corner; *Stampland* image of woman's eyes; *Postmodern Design* Roman Caps alphabet) • *ColorBox* Cat's Eye ink (Black, Chestnut) • *Postmodern Design* Walnut Ink Crystals• Glue stick

INSTRUCTIONS: **Envelope:** Apply walnut ink to Cream cardstock. Let dry. • Use diagram to cut out envelope. • Stamp corners with Black. • Use diagrams to cut Black cardstock with window. Glue Black cardstock in position. • Cover the solid side with Vintage Script paper. Sponge paper with Chestnut ink. Stamp DREAMS on tag with Black ink. Add Page Pebbles over letters. • Apply a thin line of glue to the top and bottom edge of the left side. Fold envelope closed. • **Tag Insert:** Cut tag from Black cardstock 2½" x 5". • Cut Cream cardstock 1¾" x 3½". Stamp "eyes" image in Black. Add the tassel and charm. • **Finish:** Insert the tag into the envelope.

Envelope Diagram

11"
3½"
Fold
7/8" 3/4" 7/8"
3⁷/8"
2" Cut Hole
3/4"
5½"

Black Window Card Diagram

1½"
3½"
Cut Hole
3³/8"
5½"

Black Tag Diagram

5"
3/4"
7/8"
Eyes Cardstock
2½"

Remember

by Judy Claxton

Walnut ink can be used to age more than paper.

MATERIALS: *Design Originals* (Collage papers #0613 Walnut Scroll, #0617 Music; Transparency sheets #0622 Beauties) • Cardstock (Black, Beige Confetti, Cream) • Scraps of Toile tissue paper • Rubber stamps (*Art Impression* Mini Clock E2537; *Postmodern Design* Carolyn's Survivor Slab VT1-106D, Walnut Ink Crystals) • Small manila shipping tag • Ribbon scraps (Beige, Black) • Brass flower shaped upholstery tack • *Li'l Davis Designs* Bubble Type Black Numbers with White type • Crochet lace flower trim • *Tsukineko* StazOn Black dye ink • *ColorBox* Creamy Brown Fluid Chalk • Sponge • *Scrap Happy* glue • Glue stick

INSTRUCTIONS: **Card:** Cut Black cardstock 5" x 9½". Fold in half. • Cut Music paper 4½" x 4¾". Glue Music paper to card. • **Collage:** Dip white flower trim into walnut ink. Let dry. • Paste scraps of toile tissue to card. • Tear diamonds from Walnut Scroll paper. Ink edges with Creamy Brown. Glue to card. • Stamp "Remember" onto scrap Beige cardstock in Black ink. Rub Black ink pad along edges of piece. Glue to card. • **Tag:** Sponge Creamy Beige onto tag. • Cut out diamonds from Music paper. Glue to tag. • Stamp Mini Clock in Black. • Place Beige ribbon around tag . Tape ends to tag back. • Remove post from upholstery tack. Glue to tag. • Add Black ribbon to tag. • Glue tag to card. **Mat:** Cut out transparency. Cut a mat to fit transparency from Beige cardstock and sponge with Creamy Beige. Cut a Black mat. Glue transparency to Beige cardstock. Glue to Black mat. • **Finish:** Glue crochet flower trim to top of card. Add bubble numbers.

Pull Out Tag for a Window Card Surprise!

1. Use a pattern to cut out the envelope.

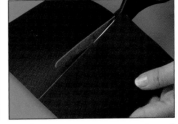

2. Use a pattern to cut out Black mat with window.

3. Center letters in window.

4. Color the stamped image.

5. Glue the stamped image to the bookmark.

6. Add a tassel.

Remembering Dad Card

by Delores Frantz

Rich colors and metal give a masculine tone to this stitched card.

MATERIALS: *Design Originals* (Window Card #0992 Small window; Vellum paper #0610 Vellum Memories; Printed Mount #0980 Water Marks) • *Jesse James* Gold and Black ¾" button • 20" *DMC* Metallic Gold embroidery floss • Gold alphabet beads • 2 Gold 4mm beads • Gold 28 gauge wire • ¹⁄₁₆" hole punch • Embroidery needle • *ColorBox* Cat's Eye Chestnut Roan ink • E6000 • Glue stick
INSTRUCTIONS: **Card:** Cut a 5¼" x 8¼" piece of vellum. Apply ink on edges. Fold in half matching the short edges. Insert card into folded vellum. Trace and cut window in vellum. Holding card front and vellum together, punch holes every ¼" along edges. Thread needle with floss and sew a running stitch through punched holes. Neatly glue floss ends inside card. • **Mount:** Thread a 4mm bead, alphabet beads and a 4mm bead on wire. Glue across card window. Glue mount over window. • **Finish:** Cut shank from button. Center and glue button in window with E6000.

Gone Fishin'

by Michele Charles

I got one "this big", but you should have seen the one that got away! Make these fun cards for the fisherman in your life. These cards are certainly the "Best Catch of the Day".

MATERIALS: *Design Originals* Collage paper (#0605 Deep Sea, #0490 Coffee Linen) • Cardstock (Gold, Blue) • Rubber stamps (*River City Rubber Works* #1484 Grandpa's Big Fish, #113B "Gone Fishin"; *Stamp Attack* #CD008C Fishing Lure; *PSX* Big Mouth Bass) • Popsicle stick • *JudiKins* dusters • *Making Memories* medium size page pebble • Brown watercolor paint • *Ranger* Distress Vintage Photo ink • *ColorBox* Black Fluid Chalk • Paintbrush • White acrylic paint • Craft knife • Glue Dots • Glue stick

INSTRUCTIONS: **Card:** Cut Blue cardstock 6½" x 8½". Fold in half 4¼" x 6½". Dry brush the inside of the card with White acrylic paint. Set aside to dry. • Cut Coffee Linen paper 4" x 6¼". Cut a section of Deep Sea paper 3¾" x 6". Dry brush Deep Sea paper with White acrylic paint. Let dry. • Cut tape measure image from Deep Sea paper. Glue tape measure image to left side of Deep Sea paper. Ink edges with Black using a small paint brush. • Glue Deep Sea paper to Coffee Linen mat. Adhere to card front with glue dots. • **Images:** Stamp Grandpa's Big Fish, Fishing lure, and Big Mouth Bass with Vintage Photo ink. Watercolor paint and cut out the images. • **Title:** Cut a popsicle stick ½" x 2". Stain with Brown watercolor paint. Stamp "Gone Fishin" in Vintage Photo ink on the center of the stick. Glue fishing lure image to edge of stick. Attach to front of card with Glue Dots. • **Finish:** Adhere "Grandpa's Big Fish" to front with glue dots. Stick page pebble over a number on the tape measure. • Adhere Bass image inside card with glue dots.

Deep Sea

by Judy Claxton

MATERIALS: *Design Originals* Collage paper (#0605 Deep Sea) • Cardstock (Beige Confetti, Rust, Sage Green, Metallic Brown) • *Stampers Anonymous* Fish Legend P1913 • *K&Company* Life's Journey Domed Typewriter Keys • *Tsukineko* StazOn Black ink • *ColorBox* Fluid Chalk ink (Burnt Sienna, Yellow Ochre, Warm Green, Creamy Brown) • *ColorBox* stylus • Copper, White, Red gel pens • Glue stick

INSTRUCTIONS: **Card:** Cut Rust cardstock 5⅜" x 11½". Fold in half. • Cut Green mat 5¼" x 5¾". Glue mat to card. • Cut Brown mat 5⅛" x 5⅝". Glue to card. • Cut Deep Sea paper 5" x 5½". • **Collage:** Cut out measure along with rope border. Glue strip to card. Add typewriter number. • Cut Green mat 3¼" x 3¾". Glue to center of card. • Cut Beige Confetti cardstock 3⅛" x 3½". • **Finish:** Stamp Fish Legend on Confetti with StazOn Black ink. Sponge edges with Yellow Ochre, Burnt Sienna and Creamy Brown ink. • Use the stylus with a foam tip to color in the fish with Warm Green ink. Use Copper and White gel pens to add lines to the central fish. Glue to card. • Cut out fish and tear coral from Deep Sea paper. Sponge edges with Creamy Brown ink. Glue to card.

1. Paint fish paper with a wash of White acrylic paint.

2. Color stamped images.

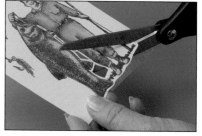

3. Cut out the images.

Nostalgia Revisited

Sail Journey

by Judy Claxton

This card sails right into the heart of anyone who loves boats. Collaging this beautiful composition will steer your creativity to the next port of call.

MATERIALS: *Design Originals* (Collage papers #0581 Little Boys, #0593 Hemispheres; Mount #0991 Large White; Transparency sheet #0556 Word Tags, #0620 Seaside) • Cardstock (Light Blue, Dark Blue, Beige) • Charms (Sea gull, Compass, Sailboat) • Old tape measure • Jute • Blue eyelet • *K&Company* Life's Journey Domed Typewriter Keys • Fine line Gold embossing powder • *Postmodern Designs* stamps (Captain Slab TR1-101D, Wood Grain Large GN5-102E) • *ColorBox* (Fluid Chalk ink Creamy Beige, Bisque, Smoke Blue; Gold pigment ink) • Sponge • *Tombow* Mono Multi Liquid glue • Glue stick

INSTRUCTIONS: **Card:** Cut Blue cardstock 6½" x 11½". Fold in half. • Cut Dark Blue mat 5½" x 6¼". Glue mat to card. • Cut Hemispheres paper 5¼" x 5⅞". Sponge edges with Creamy Beige and Bisque ink. • **Collage:** Tear sailor boy from Little Boys paper. Sponge with Creamy Beige ink. Glue in place. • Glue tape measure to bottom of the card. Tape ends behind the paper. • Emboss "Captain" from Captain slab with gold on Light Blue cardstock. Cut out closely and glue in place. • **Mount:** Use Tombow glue to adhere jute to mount. Let dry. • Cut Beige cardstock to back mount. Sponge with Bisque ink. • Cut a Light Blue tab ¾" x 1½" for the mount. Stamp with Wood Grain and Blue ink. Glue to back of mount. • Glue "journey" and "sailboat" transparencies together and tape to the back of the mount. Tape Beige mat behind transparency. Position mount on Hemisphere paper and set eyelet. • **Finish:** Glue Hemisphere paper to card. Glue charms to mount. Adhere "SAIL" from Typewriter Keys alphabet at the top of the card.

Brother

by Delores Frantz

Enhance any card with a simple buckle and grosgrain ribbon. You can change the appearance of any metal buckle by embossing it in your favorite color.

MATERIALS: *Design Originals* (Window Card #0992 Small window; Collage paper #0606 Sea, Sky and Shore, #0478 Green Linen; Printed Mount #0986 Color Game; Transparency sheet #0625 Memories) • 4" Navy Blue ⅜" grosgrain ribbon • *Dritz* Fray Check • Antique Silver ⅞" buckle • 5 Antique Silver eyelets • ⅛" hole punch • Eyelet tools • E6000 • Glue stick

INSTRUCTIONS: **Card:** Cut Green Linen 4" x 5¼". Cut window to fit card. Glue to card front. • Cut Sea, Sky and Shore paper 3¾" x 5". Cut a window to match the card. Glue to card front. • **Mount:** Cut ribbon 2½" long. Cut a point in the end. Apply Fray Check to raw edges. Set an eyelet near point. Slide buckle on ribbon. Glue to right side of card. Glue 1¼" length of ribbon to left side of card. Glue the transparency in mount. Use eyelets to attach the mount to the card.

CD Decor
by Randi Lewis

Put those spare CDs to use in this beautiful altered art piece. Use as an accent on a scrapbook page, on a card front, or put it on display in your home.

MATERIALS: *Design Originals* (Mount #0989 Small Black, Transparency sheet #0556 Word Tags) • *Paper Adventures* (Embossed Rose Paper; Green paper) • Ribbon (Black, White) • *JewelCraft* assorted beads and charms • Black *Magic Mesh* • Red Liner tape • Mono Adhesive • Glue Dots • Drill

INSTRUCTIONS: Prepare CD by drilling small hole ½" from edge. **Background**: Adhere Rose and Green papers to CD using Mono Adhesive. Turn CD over and trim excess paper along the edge of the CD. • **Layer**: Cover lower half of Green paper with Black Magic Mesh. Trim excess. Lay strip of ¼" Red Liner tape over paper seam, remove backing and cover with beads. Adhere Cream ribbon over mesh seam.**Mount**: Place transparency inside the mount and seal.. Adhere 3 cabochons to mount and mount onto CD. For extra dimension, use foam dots.• **Finish**: Thread Black ribbon through filigree charm, lay across CD and secure edges in back. Tie ribbons through hole at top.

CD Art for Card Fronts

Accents and Display

Journey Journal
by Diana McMillan

Next time you are preparing for a trip or getting ready for a scrapbook class, take a few moments to collage a notebook. You will have fun making it, and then you will have a place to record the journaling for your scrapbook pages, or an interesting place to write your "technique" notes.

MATERIALS: *Design Originals* (Collage papers #0589 At the Beach, #0591 U.S. Map, #0592 World Stamps, #0593 Hemispheres, #0594 World Maps, #0601 Old Game Pieces, #0605 Deep Sea; Printed Mounts #0982 Game Pieces; Transparency sheet #0556 Word Tags) • Manila tag book • Compass face • *WireForm* Black WireMesh • *Craf-T* Decorating Chalk • Fine grit sandpaper • *JudiKins* Diamond Glaze • Memory Tape Runner • Zots 3-D

INSTRUCTIONS: **Bottom layer**: Tear a piece of Old Game Pieces and glue to the top of the notebook cover. Tear a piece of Deep Sea paper and glue to the bottom corner. Tear the aerial view of the world from World Maps and glue in the center. • **Middle layer**: Tear a piece of Hemispheres paper. Tear a hole in the center large enough to see the aerial view from the World Maps paper. Chalk edges. Roll back the edges with your finger. Adhere in place. • Tear a piece of At the Beach paper and fill in the empty space at the bottom. • **Top layer**: Cut out the words "Western Hemisphere". Chalk the edges. Adhere in place. Cut images from World Stamps and World Maps. Chalk the edges. Adhere in place. • Adhere WireMesh in place. Glue compass to cover with Diamond Glaze. • **Mount**: Sand the corner of the mount and write the word "Journal". Secure the transparency to the back of the mount. Adhere mount to cover with Zots 3-D.

More Marvelous
Creations to
Spark the Soul
and
Lift the Spirit

Flower Pot Plant Pokes

by Barbara Burnett

Spice up a potted plant with these simple to make plant sticks.

MATERIALS: *Design Originals* (Printed Mounts #0981 Diamonds, #0985 Dictionary; Transparency sheets #0624 Art Words, #0625 Memories) • 2 popsicle sticks • Seed beads (Green, Yellow) • *ColorBox* Cat's Eye Chestnut Roan ink • 24" *Artistic Wire* 24 gauge (Green, Gold) • Wood skewer or chop stick • ⅛" hole punch • Red Liner tape

INSTRUCTIONS: Stain popsicle sticks with ink. • Tape transparencies inside mounts. Tape end of popsicle stick into mount. Tape mounts closed. • Poke holes for wire. Wind wire around a skewer to form tight coils. Add beads if desired. Thread end of wire to back of mount. Coil to secure.

Journey Card

by Diana McMillan

Encourage someone facing a difficult decision. Send this "Thinking of You" card.

MATERIALS: *Design Originals* (Vellum paper #0609 Vellum Passport; Printed Mounts #0982 Game Pieces; Transparency sheet #0561 Travel) • Tan cardstock • 3 *Jest Charming* Copper hinges • 3 *Boxer* Copper brads • 3 *Making Memories* jump rings • 3 small tags • *ColorBox* Cat's Eye Chestnut Roan ink • *Craf-T* Decorating Chalk • *WackyTac* vellum tape • Memory Tape Runner • Zots 3-D

INSTRUCTIONS: **Card**: Cut Tan cardstock 5½" x 8½". Fold in half. • Tear vellum to fit front of card. Ink the edges. • **Mount**: Ink mount. Adhere transparency to the back of the mount. Adhere hinges with brads. Adhere to card with Zots 3-D. • **Tags**: Chalk tags. Ink edges. Write words. Attach to jump rings and hinges. Adhere to card.

Spice Up your Cards with this New Card Folding Technique

Are you always looking for a new card folding technique? Something to spice up the usual? Then check out these projects. They look complicated, but they are really easy to do. Each card is folded the same. At right is the inside of the Travel - Journey card.

Page 33 pictures the inside of the ABC card.

Travel – Journey Card   *by Joyce Hazen*

MATERIALS: *Design Originals* (Collage paper #0593 Hemispheres, #0547 Dictionary; Printed Mounts #0985 Dictionary; Transparency sheets #0619 Travel 2, #0558 Script; #5207 The Ephemera Book p. 7) • Manila cardstock • Vintage images • *ColorBox* Cat's Eye ink (Chestnut Roan, Gold) • *Fiber Scraps* fibers • Game piece • Turquoise marker • *Krylon* Gold leafing pen • Craft knife • Pencil • Pop Dots • Glue stick

INSTRUCTIONS: **Card:** Computer print French script on 2 pieces of Manila cardstock in Copper colored ink. Cut both pieces of cardstock 7" x 10". Fold both in half. Set one aside for inside of card. • **Outer card:** Cover non-printed side of the card with Hemispheres paper, making sure the script on the inside is right-side up. Outline fold and edges with Gold pen. • **Mount:** Outline edges of mount with Turquoise. Cut image from The Ephemera Book. Tape image to the back of the mount. Glue mount to front of card. • **Finish:** Cut Dictionary paper 2" x 5". Fold in half. Sponge with Chestnut Roan ink on both sides. • Cut transparency image from Travel 2. Glue to a piece of Manila cardstock. Glue to Dictionary paper. Adhere dictionary paper to card. Glue game piece to bottom edge of Dictionary paper. • Glue "Journey" transparency inside Dictionary paper. • **Inside card:** Accordion fold the second piece of Manila cardstock into quarters. Quarters are labeled from left to right, 1-4. • **1:** Cut an image to fit small mount. Tape image to the back of the mount. Glue mount to page. • Cut out transparency image. Position at the bottom of section 1. Trace around transparency. Cut a window. Glue transparency to the inside of the card so it will show through the window. • **2:** Cut out transparency image. Position it on section 2. Trace around it with a pencil. Cut a window. Tape transparency to the back of section 2 so it shows through the window. Mat small tags if desired. Add fibers. Adhere to section 2 with Pop Dots. • **3:** Glue image from The Ephemera Book and other vintage images in place. • **4:** Glue vintage image and "motoring" transparency to section 4. Cut out Eiffel tower transparency. Place it on section 4. Trace around it and cut out a window. Glue the transparency to the inside of the card so the image shows through the window. • **Finish:** Sponge the edges of the accordion part with Chestnut Roan ink. • Align accordion part with inside of card. Glue sections 1 and 4 to the inside of the card, making sure the accordion fold is in position according to the photo.

ABC (outside on page 32)
Checkerboard Card
by Joyce Hazen

MATERIALS: *Design Originals* (Collage paper #0530 Mom's Sewing Box, #0554 Diamonds, #0578 Vintage ABCs, #0583 Stories for Boys, #0597 Fortune Cards, #0608 Vellum Shorthand, #0614 ABCs; Printed Mounts #0980 Water Marks; Transparency sheets #0560 Objects, #0623 Games; #5207 The Ephemera Book p. 7) • Manila cardstock • 3 charms • Gold thread • *Krylon* Copper leafing pen • Craft knife • Pencil • Ruler • Pop Dots • Glue stick

INSTRUCTIONS: **Outside card**: Cut cardstock, Shorthand, and Diamonds paper 7" x 9". Sandwich cardstock between papers and glue together. Fold in half to 3½" x 9" with Shorthand inside. • **Collage front**: Cut letters from Vintage ABCs paper. Glue "B" to card. • Cut out "FUN" transparency. Tape to the back of the mount. Mat with Manila cardstock. Adhere to card. • Cut out tape measure from Mom's Sewing Box paper. Glue to bottom of card. Ink the fold and the card edges with Copper. • Adhere "A" and "C" to card with Pop Dots. • **Insert**: Cut Checkerboard and cardstock 7" x 9". Glue together. • Fold in half. Accordion fold in quarters. • Cut slits and windows according to diagram. • **Inside card**: Mark the position of images by tracing window openings onto card. Glue images in place. • **Finish insert**: Create mountain and valley folds. Cut strips of cardstock ½" x 2¼". Fold in quarters and glue in place to make hinges on the back of the insert. Hang charms from hinges. • Glue insert end flaps to the edges inside the card.

Create the look of 3 dimensional blocks when you accordion fold and cut this checkerboard paper.

Hinge Pattern
Cut 3

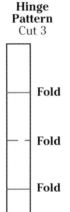

Fold

Fold

Fold

1. Fold paper in quarters.

2. Cut windows and slits with a craft knife.

3. Hang charms.

Checkerboard Cutting Diagram

Folding Key for Checkerboard

Valley Fold — · — · — · —

Mountain Fold - - - - - - -

Slit ———————

Checkerboard Hinge Diagram

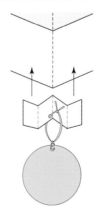

Punch hole and tie charm to hinge. Glue hinge above slit.

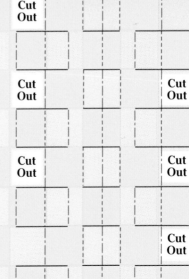

Ho Ho Ho
by Delores Frantz

Toys for Boys is an excellent choice for a Christmas background. These images also make nice gift tags and envelope seals.

MATERIALS: *Design Originals* (Window Card #0994 Three Windows; Collage paper #0582 Toys for Boys; Printed Mounts #0987 Vintage Books; Transparency sheet #0626 Holidays 2) • Dark Blue cardstock • 36" of Gold cord • 2 Gold 1" snowflake charms • 12 Gold brads • Gold Leaf pen • Ruler • 1/8" hole punch • Glue stick
INSTRUCTIONS: **Card**: Using ruler as a guide, apply Gold pen to edges of card. • Cut a 3⁷⁄₈" x 8¾" mat of Blue cardstock. Cut holes to match windows. • Cut a 3⁵⁄₈" x 8½" mat of Toy paper. Cut 3 windows to match card front. • Glue mats to card front. • **Mounts**: Cut Blue mats 2¼" x 2¾" for mounts. Trace and cut windows in Blue mats. • Stack mounts, transparencies and Blue mats. Attach brads in corners. Glue mounts over card windows. • **Finish**: Tie the Gold cord around card fold. Thread the charms on tails and tie a knot to secure.

*Special Cards
for
Special People*

Beaded Snowflake
by Delores Frantz

Let it Snow! This crystal snowflake looks so elegant against the music paper, it will set you singing while you make this wonderful card.

MATERIALS: *Design Originals* Collage papers (#0566 Music, #0567 French Horn, #0572 Green Holly) • Dark Moss Green cardstock • Nylon beading thread • Crystal Beads (twelve 6mm, 24 bugle, 30 mini pony) • 22 and 28 gauge Silver wire • Circle templates (3" and 3¼") • Glue stick
INSTRUCTIONS: **Card**: Cut Dark Moss Green card 5¾" x 9". Score and fold in half matching short edges. Cut a 3" hole in the center of the card. • Cut 2 pieces of Music paper 4¼" x 5½". Cut a 3¼" hole in the Music papers. Glue one Music paper to the front of the card. • Cut 4 leaf clusters from Green Holly paper. Glue to card. • **Snowflake**: Twist three 5" pieces of 22 gauge wire together at their center. Bend spokes out. Thread beads on one spoke. Bend a loop in the wire end to secure beads. • Wrap a 2" piece of 28 gauge wire around the spoke and between the bugle and 6mm bead. Thread a bugle and mini pony bead on each end. Bend loop in wire ends. Repeat for remaining spokes. • Tie nylon thread to opposite spokes of snowflake. Center snowflake in the card opening. Tape thread inside the front of the card so the snowflake is suspended in the opening. • **Finish**: Glue second Music paper to the inside of the card front to hide tape and thread. • **Envelope**: Cut outside of envelope from French Horns paper and lining from Music. Place envelope and lining papers back to back. Glue only top flaps together. • Score, fold side flaps. Fold bottom flap up and glue to side flaps. Fold top flap down.

Get in the Spirit

Santa Card & Envelope
by Delores Frantz

Be a good elf and get your cards done before Santa comes down the chimney! This Santa card makes it so easy, you will have a merry time making it.

MATERIALS: *Design Originals* (Collage papers #0569 Santas, #0571 Red Holly, #0549 Shorthand) • Dark Blue cardstock • 40" of Gold cord • 4 Gold eyelets • *EK Success* Clay Christmas Greetings • ⅛" hole punch • Eyelet tools • Foam tape • Pop-Dots • *Scotch* tape • Glue stick

INSTRUCTIONS: **Card**: Cut Blue card 5¾" x 9". Score and fold in half matching short edges. • Cut Shorthand paper 4⅜" x 5⅝". Cut Santa paper 4" x 4½". • Cut holly image from Santa paper. Glue to Dark Blue cardstock. Cut around image leaving ⅛" of Blue showing. • **Mat**: Glue Santa paper to Shorthand paper. • Set eyelets. • Tape end of Gold cord to back of mat. Thread through eyelets to border Santa paper. Glue mat to card. • **Finish**: Adhere holly with Pop Dots. Adhere charm with foam tape. • **Envelope**: Cut outside of envelope from Shorthand paper (using the pattern on page 36) and lining from Red Holly. Place envelope and lining papers back to back. Glue only top flaps together. • Score and fold side flaps. Fold bottom flap up and glue to side flaps. Fold top flap down. Cut out Santa image. Glue to the envelope.

Basic Envelope Pattern - Top Flap

Basic Envelope: Cut outside of envelope paper and lining. Place envelope and lining papers back to back. Glue only top flaps together. • Score and fold side flaps. Fold bottom flap up and glue to side flaps. Fold top flap down.

Fold

The Handmade Envelope... the Last Layer

Handmade cards are wonderful gifts. Make them even more special with a matching envelope. It's easy to do, and the result is really beautiful.

Making an Envelope

1. Glue or Xyron the 2 papers together as shown.

2. Draw the pattern or make and use a template.

3. Fold and glue the envelope.

Fold   **Fold**

Fold

Inside Flap

Noel
by Delores Frantz

Look at these wonderful new ways to print titles! Hammered bottle caps form a textured frame for Noel, while wires thread beaded letters together for a very merry card.

MATERIALS: *Design Originals* (Collage papers #0571 Red Holly, #0550 Tea Dye Script, #0496 TeaDye Alphabet; Legacy Cuts #0504 Green Christmas, #0505 Red Christmas) • Cardstock (Deep Red, Cream) • *Magic Mesh* • 4 Bottle caps • *Marvy* 1" circle punch • *Fiskars* stamp scissors • Rubber mallet • Pad of newspaper • Foam tape • Glue stick

INSTRUCTIONS: **Card:** Cut Cream card 5¾" x 9". Score and fold in half matching short edges. • Cut Red cardstock 4⅜" x 5⅝" with stamp scissors. Cut Script paper 4⅛" x 5⅜". • Cut images from Legacy Cuts. Layer and glue to card. • **Finish:** Cut mesh 1" x 5⅜". Adhere to card. • Place bottle

Create Truly Unique Titles for Your Season's Greetings

Tape beaded wire to the back of the mount.

Merry Christmas
by Delores Frantz

MATERIALS: *Design Originals* (Collage papers #0566 Music, #0571 Red Holly, #0572 Green Holly; Mount #0991 Large White) • White cardstock • Alphabet beads • Four *7gypsies* Silver wire double spirals • 22 gauge Silver wire • Glue stick

INSTRUCTIONS: **Card:** Cut White card 5¾" x 9". Score and fold in half matching short edges. • Cut Green Holly paper 3⅞" x 5⅝". Glue to card. • Cut Music paper 5⅝" x 8¾". • Cut a 2⅜" x 3" rectangle in card front cutting through all three layers. • **Mount:** Cut mount apart at hinge. Cover both sections with Red Holly paper. Mat mount on White cardstock. • **Finish:** Glue beads together and thread on wire. Twist loops in wire. Secure beaded wire to the back of one mount. across opening in card front. • Glue beaded mount to card front. • Glue spirals to corners of mount. • Glue other half of mount inside. • **Envelope:** Cut outside of envelope from Music paper and lining from Red Holly. Place envelope and lining papers back to back. Glue only top flaps together. • Score and fold side flaps. Fold bottom flap up and glue to side flaps. Fold top flap down.

cap with top up on a pad of newspaper. Flatten bottle cap by tapping with a rubber mallet. The edges will flare and curl towards the top. Punch letters from TeaDye Alphabet paper. Glue inside caps. • **Envelope**: Cut outside of envelope from TeaDye Script paper and lining from Red Holly. Place envelope and lining papers back to back. Glue only top flaps together. • Score and fold side flaps. Fold bottom flap up and glue to side flaps. Fold top flap down.

Hammer bottle caps until flat and adhere a round alphabet letter to the bottle cap.

....

Joy
by Delores Frantz

Add extra joy to the holiday with this attractive card and matching envelope, or make an angelic card for a special friend.

MATERIALS: *Design Originals* (Collage papers #0570 Diamonds with Holly, #0549 Shorthand) • Deep Red cardstock • Gold charm or button • 30" of Gold cord • 1" circle template • Glue stick
INSTRUCTIONS: **Card**: Cut Red card 5¾" x 9". Score and fold in half matching short edges. • Cut Diamonds paper 4¼" x 5⅝". Glue Diamonds paper to card. • **Finish**: Cut a 1" circle at center of card cutting through both layers. • Cut letters from cardstock. Glue "O" over cutout on card front. With card closed, glue charm in center of "O". Tie cord around card fold. • **Envelope**: Cut outside of envelope from Shorthand paper and lining from Diamonds. Place envelope and lining papers back to back. Glue only top flaps together. • Score and fold side flaps. Fold bottom flap up and glue to side flaps. Fold top flap down.

Angels
by Delores Frantz

MATERIALS: *Design Originals* (Collage papers #0565 Christmas Collage, #0567 French Horns, #0568 Angels Tapestry; Mount #0991 Large White) • Moss Green cardstock • Moss Green paper • 1⅝" Gold bow charm • 4 Gold brads • E6000 • Glue stick
INSTRUCTIONS: **Card**: Cut Moss Green card 5¾" x 9". Score and fold in half matching short edges. • Cut Angel paper 4¼" x 5½". • **Mount**: Cut mount apart at hinge. Cover one mount with French Horn paper. • Cut a Moss Green mat 3⅝" x 3⅝". Glue mat to mount. • Tear angel image from Christmas Collage paper. Glue in place. Add brads. • **Finish**: Glue mount to card. Adhere charm with E6000. • **Envelope**: Cut outside of envelope from Moss Green paper and lining from Angel paper. Place envelope and lining papers back to back. Glue only top flaps together. • Score and fold side flaps. Fold bottom flap up and glue to side flaps. Fold top flap down.

Angel Card   *by Diana McMillan*

Handmade cards are appreciated more than store bought ones. This trio is so easy to make, you will have time to do several.

MATERIALS: *Design Originals* (Window Card #0994 Three windows; Printed Mount #0987 Vintage Books; Transparency sheet #0626 Holidays 2) • Green cardstock • *Krylon* Gold ink • Memory Tape Runner • Zots 3-D

INSTRUCTIONS: **Card**: Cut Green cardstock 3⅝" x 8⅝". Cut 3 windows in the Green cardstock to match windows in card. Ink edge of Green cardstock with Gold. • **Mounts**: Ink the edges of the mounts. Adhere the transparencies to the back of the mounts. Adhere to Green cardstock with Zots 3-D. • **Finish**: Adhere Green cardstock to card with Zots 3-D.

Merry Christmas Card
by Delores Frantz

MATERIALS: *Design Originals* (Window Card #0993 Large window; Printed Mount #0987 Vintage Books; Transparency sheet #0626 Holidays 2) • 1 Gold bow charm • *Krylon* Gold leafing pen • Ruler • Double-sided tape • E6000 glue

INSTRUCTIONS: **Card**: Using ruler as a guide, apply Gold pen to the edges of the card. • **Mount**: Cut mount apart and ink edges with Gold. Adhere transparency to the back of the mount. Adhere mount in place. • **Finish**: Adhere charm with E6000.

A Transparency Image, Watchmaker Tin, Holly and Ribbon Create... A Lovely Tree Ornament

Christmas Ornament   *by Lisa Vollrath*

   This elegant ornament is so easy to make, you will want an entire set for yourself. Be sure you make enough to share with friends.

MATERIALS: *Design Originals* Transparency sheet (#0626 Holidays 2) • Watchmaker tin • *Offray* sheer Red wire-edge ribbon • Silk holly pick • 3" Gold Wire • *Xyron* adhesive • E6000
INSTRUCTIONS: **Lid**: Trim transparency to fit inside lid and adhere with Xyron. • **Ribbon**: Wrap ribbon around outside of tin. • Form a ribbon loop. Wrap the wire around the ribbon to secure. Tack with E6000. Peel leaves from silk holly and glue to tin around loop. Glue berries around base of loop. Trim tails as desired.

Boo Card
by Delores Frantz

MATERIALS: *Design Originals* (Window Card #0993 Large window; Printed Mount #0983 Tapes; Transparency sheet #0626 Holidays 2) • Rust cardstock • 4 upholstery nails • 3 Black ⅛" eyelets • *Remember When* Black 3-D letters • ⅛" hole punch • Eyelet tools • Glue stick • E6000 glue

INSTRUCTIONS: **Card**: Cut Rust cardstock 4¼" x 5½". Cut window to fit card. • Tape transparency to the front of the Window card. Set aside. • **Mount**: Glue mount in place on Rust cardstock. Cut tops off upholstery nails. Adhere to mount with E6000. • **Finish**: Glue tags and set eyelets. Add letters with E6000. • Glue Rust card to Window card, sandwiching transparency between.

CD Wall Hanging

by Lisa Vollrath

Just for fun, collage some CDs in your favorite theme. Play with some wire and beads to create a unique decoration.

MATERIALS: *Design Originals* (Printed Mount #0983 Tapes; Transparency sheets #0622 Beauties, #0625 Memories) • Vintage wooden ruler • CD • Mini CD • Ivory mulberry paper • Gold *Artistic Wire* 22 gauge • Assorted glass beads • *Making Memories* square Silver eyelets • Eyelet setter and hole punch • *Nostalgiques* ruler stickers • Skewer • Drill and small drill bit • *Xyron* adhesive • Glue stick

INSTRUCTIONS: **Prepare parts**: Drill holes in the top and bottom of both CDs. • Punch holes in the long sides of a small Tapes mount and in the short sides of a Tapes tag. Set eyelets into holes in mount and small tag. • **Collage**: Run transparencies through a Xyron. Collage mulberry papers, transparencies, and ruler stickers onto CDs. • **Finish**: Tape transparency to the back of the small mount. • Wrap wire around ruler and through top hole of large CD, threading beads on wire as desired. When CD is securely attached, thread wire down front of CD through center hole, filling with beads and wrapping around a skewer to create curls as desired. Attach small mount, small CD and tag in a similar manner, threading with beads and curling as desired. Wire several large beads to the bottom of the small tag.

From Pop Art to Nostalgic Art Layers Are Great!

Edwardian Ornament
by Lisa Vollrath

If you are looking for a softer, more feminine bit of home decor, here's an elegant one. Hang it on the wall in the guest room or grace the wall of the parlor.

MATERIALS: *Design Originals* Transparency sheet (#0622 Beauties) • Watchmaker tin • *Offray* ribbon (Pink satin, sheer) • Assorted Silver and Crystal beads • White ostrich feather • Silver head pins and eye pins • Round-nose pliers • Drill and small drill bit • *Xyron* adhesive • E6000

INSTRUCTIONS: **Prepare watchmaker tin**: Drill 1 hole in the top, and 3 evenly spaced in the bottom. • **Lid**: Trim transparency to fit inside lid and adhere with Xyron. Set lid aside. • **Beads**: Thread small Silver bead onto head pin and insert into top hole from inside tin. Slide large bead onto pin and wrap remainder around round-nose pliers to create loop. Repeat with three lower holes, threading beads on pins as desired. Create three dangles on Silver eye pins using crystal beads, and attach to loops. • **Finish**: Thread ribbon through top loop and tie in knot. Tie a bow from ribbon and glue to the top of the tin in front of the bead. Fill tin with ostrich feather.

Bottle Caps and Microscope Slides Morph into Incredible Jewelry

Bottle Cap Bracelet

by Lisa Vollrath

Art is fun to own and even more fun to wear. Turn old bottle caps into a trendy bracelet, or make a unique necklace with microscope slides.

MATERIALS: *Design Originals* Transparency sheets (#0621 Children, #0625 Memories) • Chain bracelet • Silver jump rings • Bottle Caps • Assorted rhinestones • Beads (Pink crystal, star-shaped, Pink seed) • Silver head pins • Pliers • *Dremel* and drill bit • Mallet • E6000

INSTRUCTIONS: **Place bottle caps** on hard surface and pound with mallet until rim rolls back. Drill hole in rims with Dremel. Cut transparencies to size of bottle cap and glue to inside with E6000. Decorate with rhinestones and set aside to dry. • **Thread jump rings** through holes in bottle caps and attach to bracelet, spacing evenly. • **Make dangles** by stringing a seed bead, crystal bead, and seed bead on eye pin. Make another group of dangles with a seed, star, and seed bead on eye pin. • Attach dangles to bracelet between bottle caps, alternating crystal with star dangle. Loop the top of the dangle pin through the bracelet and bend to close.

Journey to Paris

by Lisa Vollrath

MATERIALS: *Design Originals* Transparency Sheets (#0619 Travel 2, #0622 Beauties) • 2 Microscope slides • Silver metal tape • Black leather cord • 2 pieces of Silver wire 3" long • Silver eye pin • Key charm • 1 Red glass bead • 2 Red seed beads • Pliers • *Xyron* adhesive

INSTRUCTIONS: **Run transparencies** through the Xyron and collage onto one microscope slide. Cover with a second slide, sandwiching collage between glass. • **Create loops** in the center of each piece of Silver wire. • **Tape slides together** with Silver metal tape, positioning wire loops at top center and bottom center of slides as you work. The wire tails will hide under the Silver tape. Burnish tape to slides with thumbnail. • **Slide seed beads** and glass bead onto eye pin, clip and create loop. Attach to bottom loop of slide. Attach key charm to bottom loop on beads. • **String** the finished slide pendant onto the leather cord and knot at the desired length.

"Come and Play with Us" ...What an Irresistible Invitation!

Game Pieces, Slide Mounts, Transparency Sheets and Bottle Caps Reign Here

Come and Play with Us

by Lisa Vollrath

Take a break from the usual valentine or "thinking of you" card with fresh ideas from the "Girls will be Girls" or "Boys will be Boys" cards. "Come and Play with Us" certainly sounds like an invitation, and the game pieces assure a good time. If you have a sister, she will be having a birthday. Why not send the "sisters" card, "ladies" card, or personalize a birthday card just for her? These cards are winners!

MATERIALS: *Design Originals* (Window Card #0993 Large window; Printed Mounts #0986 Color Game; Transparency Sheet #0623 Games) • Game pieces • *Li'l Davis* Red wooden letters • Glue stick • E6000 glue
INSTRUCTIONS: **Card:** Glue bingo card to card with glue stick. Trim from window. • **Mount:** Adhere transparency to back of mount. Glue to card over window. • **Finish:** Use E6000 to adhere letters and game pieces to card.

Girls Will Be Girls

by Lisa Vollrath

MATERIALS: *Design Originals* (Window Card #0993 Large window; Printed Mounts #0984 Vintage Script, #0987 Vintage Books; Transparency sheet #0621 Children) • *Memories* Rose dye ink pad • Pink silk ribbon • Dried pansy • Heart-shaped button • Glue stick • Pop Dots
INSTRUCTIONS: **Card:** Apply Rose ink to card direct to paper. Let dry. • **Mount:** Adhere transparencies to the backs of mounts. Wrap large mount with silk ribbon and tie in bow at the lower right corner. Glue to the card over window. • Adhere small mount to card with Pop Dots, layering over large mount. • **Finish:** Glue pansy and button to card.

Boys Will Be Boys

by Lisa Vollrath

MATERIALS: *Design Originals* (Window Card #0993 Large; Printed Mounts #0984 Vintage Script, #0985 Dictionary; Transparency sheet #0621 Children) • *Fresco* Amaretto Truffle dye ink pad • Bottle cap • Star-shaped confetti • Rusty key • Metal gear • Brown ticket • *DMC* Blue pearl cotton • Pop Dots
INSTRUCTIONS: **Card:** Apply Amaretto Truffle ink to card direct to paper. Let dry. • **Mounts:** Adhere transparencies to backs of mounts. Glue large mount to card over window. Apply small mount to card with Pop Dots, layering over large mount. • **Finish:** Glue ticket, gear, bottle cap and key to card. Glue Blue star to center of bottle cap. Tie pearl cotton through key and glue tails to small mount.

Rules for Life Memory Box
by Denise Parr

Collage a positive message of love and support for someone you love in a unique container - it's a comic book tin!

MATERIALS: *Design Originals* (Collage paper #0497 TeaDye Letters, #0577 School Days, #0578 Vintage ABCs, #0579 ABCs Dictionary, #0580 School Books, #0600 Dominoes, #0601 Old Game Pieces; Printed Mounts #0980 Water Marks, #0982 Game Pieces, #0984 Vintage Script, #0985 Dictionary, #0987 Vintage Books; Transparency sheet #0624 Art Words) • *Joshua's* Lifestyle Collectibles comic book tin • *Provo Craft* (7 Bits and Pieces aluminum tins) • *Jesse James* basketball button • *Li'l Davis* Round Red alphabet pieces • 12 key tags • *Darice* sequins • *Stickopotamus* stickers (stars, cross, typewriter keys) • *Stampendous* Class A'Peels stickers • *Magenta* Pewter medallion sticker • *Offray* ribbon • Game pieces• *Small Town Treasures* miniature collection • *Craft It With Wood* wood alphabet blocks • *Rapid Design* 2" circle template R-140 • Hole punch • *Zig* Black markers • *Ranger* Pop It! Shapes foam adhesive • *Xyron* permanent adhesive • 4 *Thomas & Belts* Mounting Base surface mounts • *Art Accentz* Terrifically Tacky Tape • E6000

INSTRUCTIONS: **Outside of Box**: Run Dominoes paper through Xyron. Cover front and back of case. • Add stickers. • **Tag**: Write "Rules for Life" on a tag. Add ribbon. Adhere to cover with mounting tape. • **Round tins**: Run the following papers through the Xyron: Dominoes, School Books, ABCs Dictionary. Cut 2" circles and adhere to the inside of 6 tins. Embellish tins with stickers, sequins, beads, and miniature pieces. Adhere basketball button, round wood letters, and photographs with Pop It! foam adhesive. Glue lids to tins with E6000. • Adhere tins to lid with Terrifically Tacky tape. • **Inside of Box**: Run the following papers through the Xyron and collage to the inside of the case: Vintage ABCs, Dominoes, Old Game Pieces, School Books. • **Inside cover**: Tags: Write words on tags. Attach ribbons. Adhere to inside of lid with mounting tape. • Adhere "Life" round alphabet letters with Terrifically Tacky Tape. • **Inside box**: Tin: Write "Be Yourself" on a tag. Add ribbon. Place inside round tin. Glue lid with E6000. Adhere to box with Terrifically Tacky Tape. • Collage game pieces, blocks, and stickers on the left side, leaving room for the mounts. Adhere blocks and game pieces with E6000. • **Mounts**: Tape photos and transparencies into mounts. Tape mounts closed. • Punch holes in mounts. • Thread 4" ribbon through each mounting base. Position each base, peel and stick in place. Thread ribbon through holes in the mounts and tie.

Create Your Own 'Flip Books' of Memories and Inspirations with Slide Mounts

Great Idea !

Gather a collection of childhood memories, words of encouragement or favorite photos of a memorable event. Adhere them in mounts, punch holes in the mounts, and attach them to a base with sheer ribbon. Voila! Your own flip book.

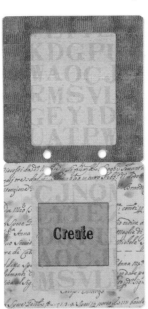

From Ordinary to Perfection In No Time At All!

Daily Diary

by Delores Frantz

Turn an ordinary notebook into a great gift in practically no time. Personalize this project with a theme and embellishments that reflect your personality. This is a fun project to do with your children or grandchildren. Let them choose their favorite materials and make their own book.

MATERIALS: *Design Originals* (Collage paper #0597 Fortune Cards; Printed Mounts #0987 Vintage Books; Transparency sheet #0624 Art Words) • 7½" x 9¾" journal • Cardstock (Black, White) • *ColorBox* Cat's Eye Chestnut Roan ink • Dark Green 27" Cord with tassels • *Remember When* Black ⅝" 3-D letters • 2 *Jesse James* Black filigree corners • 4 upholstery nails • Box clasp set • 5 Gold eyelets • Eyelet tools • ⅛" hole punch • Goop glue

INSTRUCTIONS: **Background**: Cover front of journal with Cards paper. Apply ink on edges. •**Title**: Cut Black cardstock 1¾" x 5½". Glue letters to tags. Set eyelets to attach tags. Glue to top of journal. • **Mount**: Adhere transparency in mount, back with White cardstock. Mat mount on Black cardstock. Glue to journal. • **Finish**: Cut shanks from upholstery nails. Glue heads to corners of mount. Glue filigree corners in place. Wrap tassel cord through center of book. Tie a knot against spine at the top. Glue button portion of clasp to front edge of journal. Glue remaining portion to back edge of journal. When dry, bend neck of clasp at a right angle so that it fits over button.

Games People Play - Altered Book Pages
by Lisa Vollrath

Decorate an altered book with your interpretation of "The Games People Play".

MATERIALS: *Design Originals* (Collage papers #0600 Dominoes, #0601 Old Game Pieces, #0603 Checkerboard, #0604 Target; Printed Mount #0987 Vintage Books; Transparency sheet #0623 Games) • Tan cardstock • Wood squares • Blank milk caps • Brad • Spinner arrow • *Viva Las Vegas* (Architect Alphabet stamps, face stamp) • Vintage drawings • *Memories* Black dye ink pad • Ochre *Craf-T* Decorating Chalk • *Weldbond* glue • Pop Dots

INSTRUCTIONS: **Bottom Layer**: Cover pages with Old Game Pieces paper, starting at left side. Tear edge of Tan cardstock and cover the right side of the layout. Cut corner of Checkerboard paper and glue to lower left corner of layout. Tear a small piece of Tan cardstock and layer it over the top edge of the Checkerboard. • **Middle Layer**: Cut out the center of the Target and glue it to the top right. Tear around the vintage drawings and chalk the edges. Glue to page. Cut labels from Dominoes and glue to page. • **Mounts**: Adhere transparencies to the back of the mounts. Attach to pages with pop dots. • **Finish**: Stamp letters on wood squares and glue to page. Stamp faces on milk caps and glue to page. Insert brad into spinner arrow and attach to center of target.

Phone Book
by Delores Frantz

Here's a handy notebook that fits in a pocket or purse.

MATERIALS: *Design Originals* (Collage paper #0601 Old Game Pieces; Printed Mount #0983 Tapes) • Black cardstock • Vellum • 3½" x 4½" Journal • *ColorBox* Cat's Eye Chestnut Roan ink • *Jesse James* Gold filigree charm • 4 Gold eyelets • Eyelet tools • ⅛" hole punch • Goop glue

INSTRUCTIONS: **Background**: Cover front and back of journal with Game Pieces paper. Apply ink on edges. • **Mount**: Computer print words on vellum. Glue to mount. Mat mount on Black cardstock. Set eyelets in corners. Glue to journal. • **Finish**: Glue the filigree to the mount.

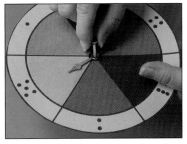

1. Attach spinner with brad.

2. Flip over and open the brad to secure.

Boys Card

by Judy Claxton

This very masculine card is perfect for birthday boys. Give it to your son, or save it for the man in your life who never quite grew up.

MATERIALS: *Design Originals* (Collage papers #0497 TeaDye letters, #0577 School Days, #0581 Little Boys, #0582 Toys for Boys, #0583 Stories for Boys; Printed Mount #0981 Diamonds; Transparency sheet #0557 Family) • Cardstock (Light Blue, Brown, Beige) • Vintage photo of small boy • Computer generated phases • *Postmodern Design* Rough Diamond image (BL12-101K) • *ColorBox* Fluid Chalk (Ice Jade, Creamy Brown) • Sponge • Mounting Tape • Glue stick

INSTRUCTIONS: **Card:** Cut Light Blue cardstock 6½" x 10½". Fold in half. • Cut Brown cardstock 5⅛" x 6⅜". Glue to front of card. • Cut TeaDye letters paper 5" x 6¼" and stamp Rough Diamond image in Ice Jade. Glue to Brown mat. • **Mount:** Sponge Ice Jade onto Diamond Slide Mount. Cut image from Stories for Boys. Tape to the back of the mount. Glue to card. • **Title:** Cut "B" from School Days paper. Cut out "oys" from transparency. Adhere transparency and vintage photo of small boy to "B". Adhere to card with mounting tape. • **Finish:** Computer print words on Beige cardstock. Cut out images from Toys for Boys and Stories for Boys papers. Sponge with Creamy Brown Fluid Chalk. Adhere to card.

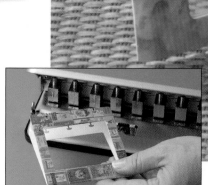

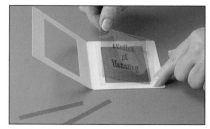

1. Punch holes in each open side of the mount with a *Rollabind* punch tool.

Photo Cube

by Stephanie Greenwood

Photo cubes fit six pictures into a small space. Make one for your desk.

MATERIALS: *Design Originals* (Printed Mounts #0980 Water Marks; Transparency sheets #0619 Travel 2, #0624 Art Words, #0625 Memories) • Paper scraps • Acid-free tape

INSTRUCTIONS: Cut out transparency images as desired. Tape transparencies and photos into mounts. • Tape mounts together to form a cube. Use paper scraps to reinforce the hinges.

2. Cut images out of transparency sheets as desired. Tape images and photos into mounts.

3. Push the mounts onto binding rings to create a terrific Star Album in minutes.